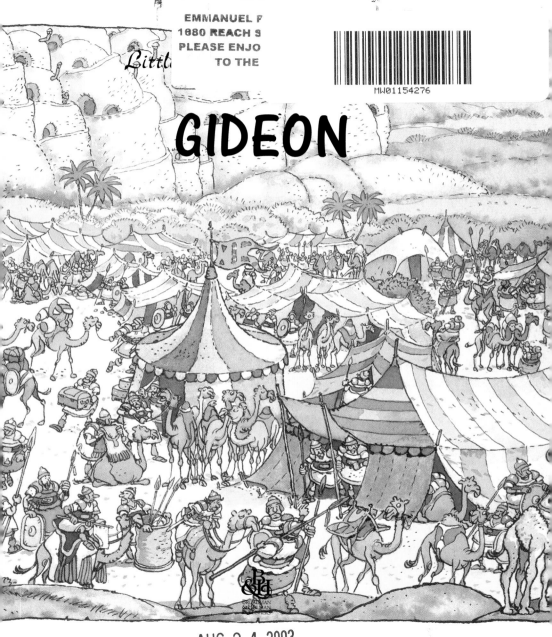

Littl

GIDEON

Dedicated to
Pedro Pérez Rollán
and to
Laura Wijnmaalen

GIDEON

Published in 2000 by
Broadman & Holman Publishers,
Nashville, Tennessee

Text copyright © 2000 Anne de Graaf
Illustration copyright © 2000 José Pérez
Montero
Design by Ben Alex
Conceived, designed and produced by
Scandinavia Publishing House

Printed in Hong Kong
ISBN 0-8054-2177-7

There once was a man named
Gideon. He was not sure about
many things.

I'm not sure if I am safe here. What do you think? Yes? No?

7

God's people were so scared of
the terrible Midianite robbers, the
Israelites had to hide in caves.

I'm not sure where I am. I'm not sure where it's safe. I'm not sure of anything!

9

The Midianites burned the Israelites' crops and stole their animals. They rode more camels than could be counted.

Can you count how many camels there were?

11

Gideon had to hide his food from the
Midianite robbers. An angel appeared
to Gideon and said, "The Lord is
with you."

This was something Gideon could be sure of. Say out loud, "The Lord is with me." You can be sure of it!

Then the angel said, "You will lead God's people against the Midianites."

The angel was sure. But Gideon wasn't so sure. What do you think? Are you sure?

15

The Lord said, "I am sending you to drive the Midianites away. Surely I will be with you."

This was one thing Gideon thought he was sure he could NOT do. But God had said SURELY he was with Gideon.

The Israelites were praying to statues instead of to God. This was very wrong. So God told Gideon to break their altar.

Gideon was STILL not sure that God would help the Israelites beat their enemies. "If the fleece is wet and the ground is dry, I'll be more sure," he prayed.

God wanted to strengthen Gideon's faith. So God made the sheepskin wet to show he would help Gideon. Do you think that made Gideon sure?

But Gideon had to be super sure. He prayed, "I'm SO unsure. Please make the sheepskin dry while the ground is wet with dew."

Then, when God did that, Gideon was super sure. What are you super sure of?

29

Before the battle, God said, "I will help you win with only 300 men. Choose the ones who drink differently than the rest. This way you can learn to be sure of me."

Can you drink water from your cupped hands? Don't spill!!

Gideon spied on the enemy camp. He heard one Midianite soldier talk about a dream he had. Gideon prayed and asked God to save them.

The Midianites were very sure that they were afraid of the Israelites! And that's what God wanted.

32

God had a plan. Gideon and his soldiers surrounded the camp and made a tremendous noise!

They held the torches in their left hands and the trumpets in their right hands.

Raise up your left hand. Raise up your right hand. Hooray for Gideon! Hooray for God!

God's people won the battle against the Midianites when Gideon became sure of what God promised him.

The people wanted to make Gideon their king, but Gideon said no. "God is your king!"

37

A NOTE TO THE big PEOPLE:

The *Little Children's Bible Books* may be your child's first introduction to the Bible, God's Word. This story of *Gideon* makes chapters 6–8 of the book of Judges spring to life. This is a DO book. Point things out and ask your child to find, seek, say, and discover.

Before you read these stories, pray that your child's little heart would be touched by the love of God. These stories are about planting seeds, having vision, learning right from wrong, and choosing to believe. Pray together after you read this. There's no better way for big people to learn from little people.

A little something fun is said in italics by the narrating animal to make the story come alive. In this DO book, wave, wink, hop, roar, or do any of the other things the stories suggest so this can become a fun time of growing closer.